Portrait
of
the Artist
with
a Red Car

Nuala Ní Chonchúir

Nuala Ní Chonchúir

Templar Poetry

First Published 2009 by Templar Poetry
Templar Poetry is an imprint of Delamide & Bell

Fenelon House
Kingsbridge Terrace
58 Dale Road, Matlock, Derbyshire
DE4 3NB
www.templarpoetry.co.uk

ISBN 978-1-906285104

Typeset by Pliny
Graphics by Paloma Violet
Printed and bound in India

For Cúán, Finn and Juno, with love

Acknowledgements

Thanks go to the editors of the following publications, in which some of these poems first appeared: *Art Now* Art Book; *Indieoma; Loqacious Placemat; Mannequin Envy; Poetry Ireland Review; Postcard Poems; Southword; The Watchful Heart - A New Generation of Irish Poets: Poems and Essays* – a Salmon anthology.

An illustrated version of the poem 'Dancing With Paul Durcan' appeared in the No Grants Gallery Writing Exhibition, Temple Bar, Dublin, May 2009.

Contents

Portrait of the Artist with a Red Car

Three Polish boys battle with their car on the garage forecourt; up they push it, down they swing it, but the car won't loosen up. It all looks as tough as waltzing with an anchor. I watch their dance through my murky windscreen, sodden in the smells of discarded food and damp; safe with an engine that always thrums to life, eventually. And I wish for better cars for all of us: for them, a Volvo estate, swift and reliable; for myself, a cherry-red Mini that will zip and glide, park in less than five arm-pulling points. Then I remember my last red car, and wonder if too much pride in its spanky redness left it a rusted heap in a Donegal scrap-yard; whether crashing it started the slow wreckage of our marriage.

Turning

I lied to my husband
and the lie lay like ashes
dry-burning my tongue,
and my tongue was like
Judas, going over to
the wrong side,
and the wrong side
was like joy – it *was* joy –
and I had to linger there,
like a woman split in half.
So I lingered long there
like a harem-bound girl,
and, in the end, the wrong side
became the right side,
and my true joy.

Dispatches

I send you messages that would make
the most liberal orthographer weep

I am impatient to get my words to you,
for you to feel their pull and depth, as I do

You send back monosyllables, brief thoughts
– your day's rhythm is not as pliable as mine –

I clutch your words, clasp and crush them,
milking their shapes for pledges, for love.

When You Are Ready

You are no ordinary Narcissus.

There is no pool that could
reflect back all you are
and keep you there, gazing.

I am your mirror, *mo ghrá*,
you glanced into me years ago
but didn't see your reflection.

It wasn't until a night in a pub
that you saw in my eyes
what you had missed before.

You grabbed my hand
under the table and stared,
fixing yourself to the spot.

Body Gifts

I give you my skin,
yellow-violet as eggshells.

I give you heartbeats,
a chest bound humming-bird.

I give you my scent,
foaming warm like yeast.

I give you lip-flesh,
made plump as twin seals.

I give you a tongue,
salt-swollen, to press into clefts.

Aubade for Extraordinary Life

In the afterglow, I watch your bear-like doze,
snout tucked under one tattooed arm.

The dawn starts its chorus, needing a witness, so
I part the curtains and see a crow toss its wings

into a hero's cloak before skydiving from phone-wires;
a cloud hangs like a balloon on a contrail string.

You father and mother me, sister and brother me,
though our heat and fervour don't talk of that,

no, it's not our nights that say all about us,
but our days and our nights, the hours dwindled

in the ordinary sharing and partings of life:
a dinner made together, lunches packed in schoolbags,

bedtime stories read, the call of each Monday morning
that sees you bound for the train, me to my desk.

All around it our love hovers, rich and sure as honey
lifted from the bee-furred heart of a sunflower.

Fruit

I am a seed-haven, spangled
with blushes and blemishes,
peel my uneven skin to get to
my pulp-plumpy core and all
the sweet glamour of the apple.

Menses

Before the butterfly days
are the fly days,
and before those,
the days of the spiders,
and along with them
come the waiting days.
The mind asks the body
if it is happening,
invisible and unseen,
a cell-dividing miracle.
The answer comes
on too many of these
long summer days,
drop by red drop.

An Unlucky Woman

I will pluck charms, dangle them
from my neck and the headboard:
rose-quartz beads and a silver turtle,
a Síle-na-Gig with gaping lips.

I will visit the rag tree at Clonfert,
pin a baby's soother to its trunk,
carry a discreet pouch of hazelnuts,
slip two gilded fish under our bed.

I will wear a Saint Gerard scapular,
the kind of thing that drips miracles,
and just maybe this army of amulets
will make my body do what it won't.

Like Esméralda, but Luckier

Like Esméralda I sit,
dark haired and white skinned,
on a versicoloured bed,
a red mohair blanket at my feet,
golden cushions at my back.

She mock-suckles her goat,
and I, an invisible baby.
Unlike Esméralda, however,
I did not choose love
with the wrong man.

Vanity

Narcissus trumpets his pleasure with himself –
if only to himself – nodding over the lake,
bowing down before his own reflection.

His image is mottled by water-scurf and flies,
like the foxing on an ancient mirror
where mercury and tin have slipped apart.

And soon his yellow freshness will slip too,
leaving a blemished likeness to gaze at, to question.

Two Children Are Threatened by a Nightingale

after Max Ernst

Max Ernst saw an eye, a nose, a bird's head,
a menacing nightingale and a spinning top
in an innocent knot of wood by his bed.

I see faces in the Rorschach-like pattern
of the curtains, a profile of a man,
snoot-nosed and Victorian, condemning us.

I dream I am in South Africa with a former lover,
we dodge bullets and buy postcards
of old houses, we touch each other's skin.

My son, worried by lightning, pulls out
the plugs all over the house; he stands still
at the window, wondering if airplanes will fall.

And I don't dare to tell him that airplanes do fall,
that people condemn, and that there is menace in more
than paintings of children threatened by a nightingale.

Other People's Children

I don't take to other people's children,
their odd manners and peculiar smells;
they are either ugly and inconsequential,
or beautiful and covetable,
but I don't want them.

And I don't want them invading my home,
staring at me like little homunculi, sly,
greedy for goodies and praise, which I give.

I'm not proud of the fact that I don't
like other people's children;
all my patience goes on loving my own,
on being a mother who gives in the *right* way.

And, I know I will fail my sons somehow,
maybe all-how, but still I try
-- try my flawed best --
or somewhere near to it at least.

Die Kinder

What loss has brought her to this,
the woman who pushes a pram
holding a child-sized doll,
its face startled and staring?

The woman wheels the pram
around the streets of Karlsruhe,
her non-child propped as a sign, maybe,
of a never-filled womb, or a baby
snatched by death or circumstance.

She looks pained but vacant,
the perfect mother to imperfect offspring,
sprung from plastic, rubber and glue.
My hard-won baby is womb-bound,
safe under skin, blood and amniotic space.

The woman holds tight to the handles,
she surveys the Christmas market
with a face worn raw from worry,
I watch her and thank God for a trio
of gifts: my sanity, my luck, my fertility.

A Sort of Couvade

There is a distance in me, a removal
from this, my last pregnancy,
few chinks let in the possibility
of a positive *coup de grace*
to end all the years of strife and faith.

I dream other people's babies,
ones who refuse to suckle,
so I hand them back to be
cauled in their mother's love,
but still my baby labours in me,
adding lanugo and vernix
to her cornucopia of miracles,
positing layers of fat
that will insulate her
when she delivers herself to us
in the cool-aired birthing suite,
borne down by my body's rhythms,
because and in spite of me.

Wrapped in a battle-dress of
grease, blood and bruising,
she will wear me like a crown
before forcing through, pulling labia taut,
and I will be present because
that is what I am made for,
I will perform a sort of *couvade*
at my only daughter's birth.

After Birth

The unbelief that we had made it,
me and this sparrow-small, soft-boiled boy
tucked in my arm on a narrow bed,
in a scratchy yellow blanket,
on a dim night ward.

I kept him by me,
glad of the nurses' neglect,
I fed him, his pursed suckle
already perfected, an expert
like my first-born.

I listened to other babies cry,
called a nurse to ask for food
and she found me two biscuits.

I fought the pain, the blood-gush,
the breaking tiredness,
too seduced and drunk on love
to waste time on sleep.

Walking Saint-Germain

On wide stalls in
the Marché Biologique,
flayed rabbits cuddle
tight, flank-to-flank;
plump pigeons coo quietly
to comfort shiny squid,
tiny as unborn babies.

On the boulevard,
under l'Atelier's awning,
two strait-laced boys
drink each other in,
sink cocktails to love
and smoke like novices;
a squat Boxer winks
at me from a doorway.

Flâneuse

On rue Mouffetard:

In a tat and toy shop, I buy
a Tour Eiffel snow-shaker,
the snow is blue glitter,
the tower, the bleu-blanc-rouge.

In the Pompidou:

Menace licks around corners here
like a misogynist's tongue;
a Buddha trails his intestines
into the beaks of birds of prey.

On the métro:

A man from Aix-en-Provence tells me
I'm pretty, like Emil Nolde's wife,
he says he's had enough of this city,
he's off home to press olives.

At the Musée Carnavalet:

Each transposed interior is manned
by a bored-faced, uniformed woman;
the Louis XV room held women once
who were powdered and iced like cakes.

On the train:

I am startled by a man
who fast-paces the carriage,
thumps the walls and screams:
'Monsieur, oh-la-la! Maman!'

The Hen Whisperer

The hen sits on the dry-stone wall,
my palms collaring her neck;
we face each other, lip to beak,
her comb and wattle jiddering.

Fingering her feathers, I cluck,
forming a burble of hen-speak:
'Remember pipping through the violet
membrane; think of your egg-tooth.'
My hands gather around her plump,
mimicking a shell, her safest place.

But this hen is having none of it;
she swells her feathers and pecks,
flusters from the wall and struts off;
she is this coop's renegade chicken,
an untameable maverick; a ne'er do well.

Dancing with Paul Durcan

I saw Paul Durcan in The Winding Stair,
fingering a book of love sonnets.
'Paul,' I said, 'your poetry is filthy with longing.'
He said, 'Would you like to dance?'

So breast to chest we turned a Durcanesque
polka of long poems and harem-scarem
happenings around the bookstacks.

And, oh, the heft of him.

'I won't be falling in love with you,' I said,
'That's OK,' Paul murmured, 'love's not
looking for me at the moment. We've fallen out.'

Our bodies collided into man-woman as we swung,
our clothes and skin sewn into each other,
our legs a kicking chorus of dance, dance, dance.

Paul spun me down the winding stairs,
up across the bow of the Ha'penny Bridge,
and, spinning together, all our pages flew.

Saint Patrick's Day, Achill Island

'Jamesie,' she says to me, from the chair,
'put the green frock on me today,
I'm feeling powerful festive.'
'I will, Dolly,' says I, 'it's the one colour
that brings up the gold in your hair.'
'Don't cod me,' she roars, 'the hair's a disaster.'

We settle down, watch the parade on RTÉ,
and drink six bottles of porter apiece.
'This is the life, Dolly, hah?' I say,
but there isn't a gug out of her;
all I hear are gulls and the hum-thrum
of a tractor going down the boreen.

The Virgin Statue

And she will still be there, tall as a toddler,
static in her wooden cave, table-bound,
queening it over the piano where mice tinker,

over an empty, many-coverleted bed,
the clock, hollowed out of chimes,

over a sea of mats, the black-and-white TV
– conduit to this century – blank-screened, silent.

She must be there still, eyes mad with sorrow,
missing, maybe, the mingle of fried spuds and Coty,
the ghosts of dogs, the May-long worship at her shrine.

Dream after a Reading

The poet takes me into his bed
and I undress him;
his back is a Colosseum
of stacked tattoos, colourful badges
underscored with script:

'And O she was the Sunday in every week'.

The poet's limbs are thick, manly,
he drools kisses into my mouth,
but still I like him;
I wake with the heft of him
heavy and hard between my legs.

Woman and Cosmetics

after Wayne Thiebaud

This is my canvas:
my mother's legacy of white skin,
my father's of fertile girth.

All my life I have tried to alter
what was decreed in the womb,

With five shades of lipstick:
Ice Pink, Rosé Requinqué, Macao,
Café Latté, Lady Bug,

With fake-flesh concealer and
pots of eyeshadow, bruise-blue,

I brush and rub, pencil and shade,
making a more palatable woman
of the woman that I am.